The Heinemann Illustrated Encyclopedia

Volume 1

Aar-Bir

Heinemann
LIBRARY

First published in Great Britain by Heinemann Library
Halley Court, Jordan Hill, Oxford OX2 8EJ
a division of Reed Educational and Professional Publishing Ltd.

OXFORD MELBOURNE AUCKLAND
JOHANNESBURG BLANTYRE GABORONE
IBADAN PORTSMOUTH NH (USA) CHICAGO

Series Editors: Rebecca and Stephen Vickers
Author Team: Rob Alcraft, Catherine Chambers, Jim Drake,
Fred Martin, Angela Royston, Jane Shuter, Roger Thomas,
Rebecca Vickers, Stephen Vickers
Reading Consultant: Betty Root

Photo research by Katharine Smith
Designed and Typeset by Gecko Ltd
Printed in Hong Kong by Wing King Tong

02 01 00 99 98
10 9 8 7 6 5 4 3 2 1

ISBN 0 431 09052 1

British Library Cataloguing in Publication Data.

The Heinemann illustrated encyclopedia
  1. Children's encyclopedias and dictionaries
  I. Vickers, Rebecca II. Vickers, Stephen, 1951–
  032

ISBN 0431090629

Acknowledgements:
Cover: The cover illustration is of a male specimen of *Ornithoptera goliath*, commonly called the
Goliath Birdwing. Special thanks to Dr George C. McGavin and the Hope Entomological Collections,
Oxford University Museum of Natural History.

Ancient Art and Archicture: p21m. **BBC Natural History Unit:** p31t (Rico & Ruiz). **Steve Benbow:**
p37. **Bridgeman Art Library:** p24t. **J. Allan Cash Ltd.:** pp6b,10, 27, 32, 34b, 36, 45, 46. **John Cleare
Mountain Camera:** p9b. **Dee Conway:** p33t. **Hulton Getty:** pp6t, 38t, 47r **The Hutchison Library:**
pp7, 8, 11, 23, 28 (J.G.Fuller), 35. **Oxford Scientific Films:** p4; John Beatty – p26; G.I. Bernard – pp16t,
40b; Mary Chillmaid – p19t; Clive Bromhall – p20l; Stephen Dalton – p39t; E.R. Degginger – p20r; John
Downer – p19b; Michael Fogden – p18t; D.G. Fox – p44t; C.W. Helliwell – p16b; Manfred Kage – p30b;
Lon E. Lauber – p22; Andrew Lister – p17; James M. McCann – p41b; Stan Osolinski – pp12, 44b;
Partridge Films – p39b; Leonard Lee Rue III – pp41t, 42; David Shale – p43b; Alastair Shay – p31b;
Survival Anglia p25 (Michael Pitts), p18b (Alan Root); David Thompson – p43t; Akira Uchiyama – p15t;
Babs & Bert Wells – 15b; Belinda Wright – p5. Potton Homes: p21b. **Science Photo Library:** pp9t
(John Mead), 30t (A.B. Dowsett), 40t (Geospace). **The Tate Gallery:** p24b. **Tony Stone Worldwide:** p47
(Ed Pritchard); 38b (Richard H. Smith). **Werner Forman Archive:** p21t.

Every effort has been made to contact copyright holders of any material
reproduced in this book. Any omissions will be rectified in subsequent printings if
notice is given to the Publisher.

Welcome to the
Heinemann Illustrated Encyclopedia

What is an encyclopedia?

An encyclopedia is an information book. It gives the most important facts about a lot of different subjects. This encyclopedia has been specially written for children your age. It covers many of the subjects from school and others you may find interesting.

What is in this encyclopedia?

In this encyclopedia each topic is called an entry. There is one page for every entry. The entries in this encyclopedia are on:

- animals
- plants
- dinosaurs
- countries
- geography
- history
- world religions
- music
- art
- transport
- science
- technology

How to use this encyclopedia

This encyclopedia has eleven books, called volumes. The first ten volumes contain entries. The entries are all in alphabetical order. This means that Volume One starts with entries that begin with the letter 'A' and Volume Ten ends with entries that begin with the letter 'Z'. Volume Eleven is the index volume and has some other interesting information in its Fact Finder section.

Here are two entries, showing you what you can find on a page:

The See also *line tells you where to find other related information.*

This is the letter that the entry starts with.

Fact *boxes give you details about the topic.*

Did You Know? *boxes have fun or interesting bits of information.*

The Fact File *tells you important facts and figures.*

Aardvark

See also: Ant, Mammal, Termite

An aardvark is an insect-eating mammal which lives in Africa. Its name means 'earth pig' in the Dutch language.

Aardvark families

Aardvarks live separately, not in groups. The female aardvark usually gives birth to a single baby, which lives with its mother until it is six months old. Male aardvarks live on their own. The aardvark digs itself several homes, called burrows, where it sleeps during the day. Aardvarks come out to feed at night.

FOOD

Aardvarks use their 45 cm long tongue to eat termites and ants after digging into their nests, usually at night. They also like fruit.

AARDVARK FACTS

NUMBER
OF KINDS..... 1
COLOUR...... beige-grey
LENGTH.......1.5–1.9 m
HEIGHT........about 50 cm
WEIGHT.......40–65 kg
STATUS........ common
LIFE SPAN..... 10 years
ENEMIES....... dogs, pythons, lions, leopards, warthogs

This aardvark is digging into a termite mound.

Nose to smell out ants and termites. The nostrils close to keep out insects

Long ears to help keep cool

Strong tail to hit attackers

Strong claws for digging burrows, breaking into termite mounds and for protection

An aardvark

Aborigines

See also: Australasia, Australia

Aborigines were the first people in Australia. They have been there for 45,000 years. They are famous for their stories and their art.

Land and life

Aborigines live together in family groups called tribes. They had to teach themselves special skills to be able to live. Near the sea they used spears and nets to catch fish. In the deserts they were skilled at finding water and food.

Spirits and beliefs

Aborigines believe their land was created in a time they call the Dreamtime. The land is very special to Aborigines. They believe that their spirits will return to the land when they die.

European people arrived in Australia over 200 years ago. They took the Aborigines' land and sacred places. Later they tried to make Aborigines forget all about their history and beliefs.

Aborigines today

Aborigines live in all parts of Australia. Only a few still live in the old way. Gradually their sacred places are being returned to them.

Aboriginal art often tells stories of spirits and the Dreamtime.

DID YOU KNOW?

Aborigines invented the boomerang to use for hunting. If it is thrown correctly, it will return to the person who threw it.

Aboriginal women making a traditional string game pattern of a turtle, like cat's cradle.

Aeroplane

See also: Helicopter, Transport

An aeroplane is a machine that flies in the air. It has wings and an engine. Aeroplanes were invented around the same time as cars.

AEROPLANE FACTS

BIGGEST ...... Hughes H2 Hercules, wing span: 97.54 m

SMALLEST .... Skybaby, wing span: 2.18 m

FASTEST .... Lockheed 'Blackbird', 3529.56 kph

The first aeroplane

The first aeroplane to fly was built by the Wright brothers in North Carolina, USA. It flew for only 12 seconds on 17 December 1903. It had a wooden frame and was covered in cloth. Later aeroplanes were made from metal which was light and strong. They had more powerful engines, which meant they could fly faster and higher.

An early flight by Wilbur and Orville Wright.

How we use aeroplanes

Before aeroplanes were invented, journeys to other countries took months, or even years. Today huge jumbo jets carry millions of passengers and tonnes of cargo all over the world. Journeys take only a few hours. We can have holidays abroad, and meet people far away, all because of aeroplanes.

Most modern jumbo jets, like this Boeing 747, can carry over 400 passengers.

Afghanistan

See also: Asia

Afghanistan is a country in central Asia. It is dry, with cold winters. Most Afghans live on flat land in the north. In the south are mountains and deserts.

These Afghan women are winding wool.

Living and working

Many Afghans live in high mountain villages. They keep sheep, yaks and camels, and farm in the valleys. Their houses are built with mud bricks and flat roofs. They are built on the valley slopes.

Most Afghans wear traditional long robes. Women often wear veils which cover their faces. Nearly everyone eats rice. People also like tea and a yoghurt drink called *dagh*.

Afghanistan has had many years of war. This has made life very difficult. Many Afghans have left their homes to escape the fighting. Some have moved to special camps in Pakistan.

DID YOU KNOW?

The temperature in Afghanistan can go from −20 °C in winter to over 40 °C in the summer.

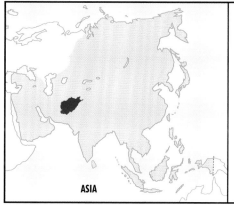

ASIA

FACT FILE

PEOPLE	Afghans
POPULATION	about 20 million
MAIN LANGUAGES	Pushtu, Persian
CAPITAL CITY	Kabul
MONEY	Afghani
HIGHEST MOUNTAIN	Noshaq – 7499 m
LONGEST RIVER	River Helmand – 1150 km

Africa

See also: Continent, Desert

Africa is the second biggest continent. It is south of Europe and the Mediterranean Sea. The Atlantic Ocean is to the west and the Indian Ocean is to the east.

The land

There are huge plains with flat or gently sloping land. The highest mountain ranges are the Atlas Mountains, the Ethiopian Highlands and the Drakensberg Mountains. The Sahara Desert takes up most of the north of Africa. The Kalahari Desert is in the south.

Climate, plants and animals

The climate in the rainforest in the centre of Africa is hot and very wet all year. There are also large areas of grassland, with some trees, called the savanna. Herds of wildebeest, zebra, antelope, elephants and other animals live in the savanna.

People in Africa

Africa is home to many different groups and tribes, who live in 53 countries. Most people live in the countryside, but there are also towns and cities. Many Africans are farmers, but Africans also work in copper, gold, tin, diamond and coal mines.

AFRICA FACTS

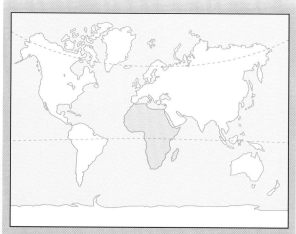

SIZE	30.2 million square km
HIGHEST MOUNTAIN	Mount Kilimanjaro – 5895 m
LONGEST RIVER	River Nile – 6700 km
LARGEST LAKE	Lake Victoria – 74,664 square km
BIGGEST COUNTRY	Sudan

Cape Town in South Africa is one of Africa's large cities.

Air

See also: Oxygen, Pollution

Air is a mixture of gases. It is invisible and has no smell, but it is very important. Without the air in the atmosphere, living things could not breathe.

What is air made of?

The main gas in the air is nitrogen. It makes up four-fifths (80%) of the air. About a fifth (20%) of the air is oxygen. When we breathe in, our bodies use the oxygen and we breathe out another gas, carbon dioxide. Burning fuels, such as coal and wood, also makes carbon dioxide. Trees and other plants use carbon dioxide and give out oxygen.

The air over the American city of Los Angeles looks hazy because of fumes from cars and factories.

This climber has climbed so high that he needs to use air from an oxygen cylinder. This helps him breathe easily where the air is thin.

Dangers to the air

Clean air helps to keep us healthy. Car engines put harmful gases into the air. This is one sort of air pollution. Smoke is another. It can hurt our lungs and make us ill.

Pollution makes the air dirty and dangerous to breathe. Cutting down trees can also harm the air because trees make oxygen.

Albania

See also: Europe

Albania is a country in south-east Europe. The east is cold, with mountains and forests. In the west, there are flat coast areas. Summers are hot and dry. Winters are warm and wet.

This is Main Street in the capital city, Tirana. Even modern buildings are built with balconies.

Living and working

Most people live in stone houses in the countryside. In one area, houses are built into the rock. They have carved wood windows and balconies.

Albanians like to eat cheese, yoghurt and meat with peppers, tomatoes and carrots. They eat olives for snacks. Farmers in Albania grow grapes, olives, cotton and tobacco.

Every year a folk music festival is held in the town of Schkodra. Some songs date back thousands of years to when Albania was ruled by Greece.

DID YOU KNOW?

Mother Teresa, the famous nun who helped the poor of India, was born and grew up in Albania.

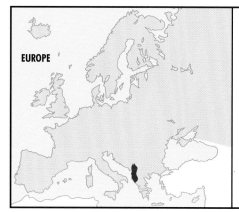

EUROPE

FACT FILE

PEOPLE........................ Albanians

POPULATION .... about 3 million

MAIN LANGUAGES .... Albanian, Greek

CAPITAL CITY.............. Tirana

MONEY....................... Lek

HIGHEST MOUNTAIN... Mount Korab – 2751 m

LONGEST RIVER.......... River Drin – 152 km

Algeria

See also: Africa, Desert

Algeria is a country in north-west Africa. It has coastal areas, deserts and mountains. Over three-quarters of Algeria is covered by the Sahara Desert, the largest desert in the world.

Living and working

Most Algerians live near the coast. Houses are painted white to reflect the hot sun. There are roof terraces where it is cooler to sleep at night.

Algerians eat a lot of lamb. They also eat flaky pastry filled with egg or meat, spices and olives, called *brik*. They have stewed spiced meat cooked with fruit, called *tadjin*. It is served with couscous, which is made from steamed wheat.

Farmers in Algeria keep 14 million sheep. Grains, citrus fruit, grapes, olives and dates are also grown. Other Algerians work producing oil or in mines.

This is an open air market in Algeria. People shelter from the sun under the arches. People wear white to reflect the sun and keep cooler. A fold of a headdress can keep dust and sand out of the nose and mouth.

DID YOU KNOW?

Algeria is well-known for its leather goods. Even motor oil is sometimes carried in pouches made of goat skin.

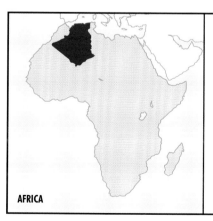

AFRICA

FACT FILE

PEOPLE	Algerians
POPULATION	about 29 million
MAIN LANGUAGES	Arabic, French, Berber
CAPITAL CITY	Algiers
MONEY	Algerian Dinar
HIGHEST MOUNTAIN	Mount Tahat – 3003 m
LONGEST RIVER	River Chelif – 725 km

Alligator

See also: Crocodile, Reptile

The alligator is a very big reptile that lives in rivers, lakes and swamps. It is a close relative of the crocodile. One type lives in south-east USA, while the other lives in south-east China. The alligator's snout is less pointed than the crocodile's, and the teeth are different.

ALLIGATOR FACTS

NUMBER OF KINDS....	2
COLOUR.....	greyish-brown
LENGTH......	up to 4 m
WEIGHT.....	up to 250 kg
STATUS.......	threatened
LIFE SPAN...	up to 60 years
ENEMIES.....	Some birds eat alligator eggs and hatchlings. People kill alligators for their skins or to control the population.

FOOD

Alligators hunt during the day. Hatchlings eat insects and frogs. Adults eat larger animals and fish.

Eyes on top of the head for hiding underwater and seeing over the water

Nostrils that close when underwater

An American alligator

Strong tail for swimming

Thick skin for protection

Strong legs and sharp claws for walking, swimming and digging

Long teeth to hold food

Alligator families

A male alligator is called a bull and a female is called a cow. Alligator babies are called hatchlings. The female builds a mound of mud and rotting leaves and lays 25–60 eggs, then puts more mud on top. She then stays close to the nest and opens it up when she hears the hatchlings squeaking.

Hatchlings sun themselves on waterside reeds.

Alphabet

See also: Language, Literature, Numbers

An alphabet is the letters or shapes that people use to write down their language. The word 'alphabet' comes from the first two letters in the Greek alphabet – 'alpha' and 'beta'.

Early alphabets

A very important alphabet was worked out in about 2000 BC in Syria. Over time, different people changed it to fit their own languages. The Greeks and Romans each used it to make their early alphabets.

The English alphabet came from the early Roman alphabet. Other languages, such as Arabic, Chinese and Hebrew, use different symbols for their alphabets.

English	Greek	Arabic
A a	A α - A	ا - • orA
B b	B β - V	ب - B
C c	Γ γ - G or Y	ت - T
D d	Δ δ - TH	ث - S or T
E e	E ε - E	ج - G or SH
F f	Z ζ - Z	ح - H
G g	H η - I	خ - K
H h	Θ θ - TH	د - D
I i	I ι - I	ذ - Z or D
J j	K κ - K	ر - R
K k	Λ λ - L	ز - Z
L l	M μ - M	س - S
M m	N ν - N	ش - SH
N n	Ξ ξ - X	ص - S
O o	O o - O	ض - D
P p	Π π - P	ط - T
Q q	P ρ - R	ظ - Z
R r	Σ σ ς - S or Z	ع - •
S s	T τ - T	غ - H or R
T t	Y υ - I	ف - F
U u	Φ φ - F	ق - K or •
V v	X χ - H	ك - K
W w	Ψ ψ - PS	ل - L
X x	Ω ω - O	م - M
Y y		ن - N
Z z		ه ة - H
		و - W,O or U
		ى - Y,I or E

These are the English, Greek and Arabic alphabets that are used today.

KEY DATES

4000 BC	The first alphabet was worked out
2000 BC	The first modern alphabet appeared
1400 BC	The Chinese alphabet
759 BC	The Greek alphabet
600 BC	The Roman alphabet
AD 700	People begin to use small letters and capital letters
AD 800	Japanese phonetic alphabet
AD 1800	The first Native American alphabet

Different kinds of letters

The 26 letters in the English alphabet come from the Roman alphabet that was used over 2000 years ago. The English alphabet has two kinds of letters. There are vowels (a, e, i, o, u) which are soft sounds. There are also harder sounds called consonants. The letters are arranged in a fixed order. This order can be used to organize words so they can be found in dictionaries, or to list names in telephone books.

Amphibian

See also: Frog, Metamorphosis, Toad

Amphibians are animals that are found all over the world, except in very cold places. Amphibians spend most of their adult life on land, but begin life in water. They return to water to lay their eggs. In the water, young amphibians breathe with their gills. Adults can breathe through their skin as well as with their lungs.

AMPHIBIAN FACTS

LIFE SPAN .. Most amphibians live from 5 to 15 years. Salamanders can live up to 50 years.

ENEMIES .... Herons, large fish and snakes. People sometimes fill in the ponds where amphibians live.

Eggs are laid in jelly to protect them and to help them float. These eggs are called spawn.

A frog has long legs for jumping and webbed back feet for swimming.

The metamorphosis of a frog

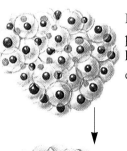

A tadpole grows in each egg.

A tadpole has a long tail which it uses for swimming.

When the tadpole has legs it is called a froglet. The tail gradually disappears.

Amphibian families

In the spring, amphibians lay many eggs in ponds and rivers. These eggs are called spawn. Baby amphibians, called tadpoles or larvae, swim in the water and breathe through gills. During the summer they develop lungs. Then they leave the water. These changes are called metamorphosis. Amphibians do not build a home, but may shelter under stones or plants.

FOOD

Small tadpoles and larvae eat water plants. As they grow they begin to eat water insects and other small creatures. Adult amphibians usually eat worms, slugs and insects.

Animal

See also: Invertebrate, Vertebrate

An animal is a living thing that can feed, move around and breed. Animals live everywhere in the world – on land, in water and in the air. Animals are divided into different groups, such as mammals, birds, reptiles, fish and insects. People who study animals are called zoologists.

Animal families

Most animals are either male or female. It takes a male and a female of the same kind of animal to produce babies. Some animals build homes to live in, but other animals wander from place to place looking for food. Some animals live alone, but others stay in groups.

LIFE STYLES

Some animals sleep during the day and hunt for food at night. They are nocturnal. Others sleep at night and look for food during the day. They are diurnal. Some small animals eat and sleep throughout the day and night.

Mammals such as these Japanese snow monkeys, and also birds, make their own heat. They are called warm-blooded.

This lizard is warming itself in the sun. Reptiles, fish and many other animals have to get heat from their surroundings. They are called cold-blooded.

FOOD

Animals either eat plants or other animals. Plant-eating animals are called herbivores. Meat-eating animals are called carnivores. Animals that eat insects are called insectivores. Animals that eat a variety of plants, insects and meat are called omnivores.

Ant

See also: Aardvark, Anteater, Insect

An ant is a small insect. It lives with other ants in a group called a colony. Some colonies have just a few ants but other colonies have thousands of ants. Ants live in all but the coldest parts of the earth.

ANT FACTS

NUMBER OF KINDS	over 10,000
COLOUR	black, brown or red
LENGTH	0.1–2.5 cm
STATUS	common
LIFE SPAN	from a few weeks to 20 years
ENEMIES	aardvarks, anteaters, birds, frogs, lizards, spiders, other insects, people

FOOD

Ants eat a wide variety of food from leaves to dead animals. As an ant chews its food, it squeezes out the sugary juice and spits out the solid bits. Ants eat day and night.

Antennae to smell, touch, taste and hear things

Strong jaws hold food, fight enemies and can lift things ten times bigger than the ant

Hard covering protects the ant's insides

Sharp claws at the end of each leg to walk up walls and the undersides of leaves and twigs

A red ant

Ant families

Each colony has three kinds of ant. The queen ant is a female who spends her whole life laying eggs. The worker ants are other females who find food, look after the queen and look after the young. Male ants die as soon as they have mated with the queen. Some colonies of ants build huge nests below the ground.

Thousands of ants worked together over many years to build this huge nest.

Antarctica

See also: Continent

Antarctica is the fifth biggest continent. It is not divided up into countries, like the other continents.

The land
Antarctica is covered by ice. Ice covers the valleys, plains and mountains. Even the sea is frozen around some of the coast.

Climate, plants and animals
Antarctica is the coldest continent. It is usually below freezing point (0 °C) all year round. In summer, the sun does not go down for several months. In winter, the sun does not appear at all for several months. Nothing grows in Antarctica except some mosses and lichens. Penguins, seals, whales and small shrimps called krill live in the ocean around Antarctica.

People in Antarctica
Roald Amundsen from Norway was the first person to reach the South Pole. He got there on 14 December 1911. Now scientists from different countries are the only people who live in Antarctica. They study the rocks, wildlife and the climate. The USA and Australia's scientific base at the South Pole is completely underground. This keeps it warm and safe from winds and storms.

ANTARCTICA FACTS

SIZE .... 14.2 million square km

HIGHEST
POINT .... the Vinson Massif − 4897 m

ICE .... 90% of the world's fresh water is in Antarctica's ice

SPECIAL
FEATURE .... the South Pole, the most southern point on Earth

This is the scientific study base "H" on Signy Island in Antarctica.

Anteater

See also: Ant, Mammal, Termite

The anteater is a mammal. There are four kinds of anteaters that live in the forests and open plains of Central and South America. The giant anteater is the biggest.

ANTEATER FACTS

NUMBER
OF KINDS 4
COLOUR ...... grey, brown, black and white
LENGTH .... up to 2 m
HEIGHT .... about 70 cm
WEIGHT ...... 20–38 kg
STATUS .... common
LIFE SPAN ..... 25 years
ENEMIES .... jaguars, people

FOOD

An anteater visits several different nests of termites or ants each time it needs to eat. It never eats all the ants in one nest, so that the food does not run out.

Colours help it hide in long grass

Long hair to keep warm and dry

Sensitive nose smells ants and termites underground

An anteater

Long, spiky, sticky tongue to catch ants deep underground

Strong claws for digging up ants and termites and for protection

Anteater families

Male and female anteaters do not live together. Anteater babies are born in pairs and live with their mother for two years, until they are grown up. An anteater does not make its own home, but will often sleep in a burrow made by another animal.

A baby anteater holds on to his mother's back while she eats.

Antelope

See also: Deer, Mammal

An antelope is a mammal with horns and hooves. It looks a bit like a deer. Most antelope live in Africa but some live in Asia and North America.

Antelope families

Female antelope and their young often live together in large groups called herds. The herd moves around in search of food. The females visit a male's territory and mate with him to produce new young. The females have only one baby at a time.

ANTELOPE FACTS

NUMBER OF KINDS....	over 100
COLOUR.....	usually brown or grey
HEIGHT.......	25 cm to 1.8 m
WEIGHT......	6.8–545 kg
STATUS........	some endangered
LIFE SPAN....	2–5 years
ENEMIES......	lions, leopards, wild dogs, wolves, coyotes, people

Horns are made of bone and are sometimes used to fight

Big ears listen out for danger

A male bontebok antelope

Strong legs help the antelope to run up to 60 kph

Hooves are like those of sheep and cattle

FOOD

Antelope eat grass and shrubs during the day. An antelope chews its food twice. It swallows the grass almost whole, then later brings it back up to chew again.

Topi antelope and young listening for danger.

Ape

See also: Mammal, Monkey

Apes are large mammals. They are closely related to human beings. There are several types, including the chimpanzee, the gorilla, the gibbon and the orang-utan. Apes live in Africa and Asia.

Ape families

Gorillas and chimpanzees live in groups called bands or troops. Gibbons live in families made up of a mother, a father and their children. Orang-utans live on their own, except that the mother looks after her baby. Apes usually have only one baby at a time. Most apes make a new sleeping platform in a tree each evening, but big male gorillas sleep on the ground.

FOOD

All apes eat fruit, leaves, insects and shoots, but some chimpanzees eat monkeys as well. Apes feed during the day.

A young chimp keeps dry on its mother's back while she drinks.

APE FACTS

NUMBER OF KINDS	13
COLOUR	black or brown. The orang-utan is reddish orange.
HEIGHT	up to 1.8 m tall
WEIGHT	heaviest ape (male gorilla) up to 275 kg
STATUS	some endangered
LIFE SPAN	20–50 years
ENEMIES	People often kill adult apes and take the babies to sell as pets. People also destroy the forests where apes live.

A gibbon

The very long thumb helps the gibbon to grip branches

Long arms are used for swinging through the trees

The gibbon has a throat sac which makes its voice very loud. Orang-utans also have this.

Feet are flexible for holding onto branches. Gibbons' toes are like extra fingers.

Architecture

See also: Art, Castle, Cathedral, Home

Architecture is the art of planning buildings. People who design buildings are called architects. Buildings have to look good and be safe and strong. They also have to be comfortable to live and work in.

Pillars have been used since ancient times to support roof beams.

The three kinds of building

Architects use three main methods for making buildings. The simplest is to build pillars or walls and put beams on top, to hold up the roof. Another way is to use arches to support the building. The third way is to build a strong frame of wood or metal and attach the walls and roof to it.

Good buildings

Even though buildings look very different now to how they did long ago, all good buildings have some things in common. A well-designed building will be just right for its job. A school will be different from a house, and a house will be different from a supermarket. Good buildings should be built using the correct materials for the job the building does.

A typical Gothic building, like this cathedral, uses arches for support.

A strong wooden frame provides the support for the wallboards and roof.

Arctic

See also: Tundra

The Arctic is the region around the North Pole. It is not a continent. Most of the Arctic is ocean that is always frozen. There are some islands in the Arctic, but most of the ice of the Arctic has no land under it. Greenland is the biggest island. Parts of North America, Europe and Asia are also inside the Arctic Circle.

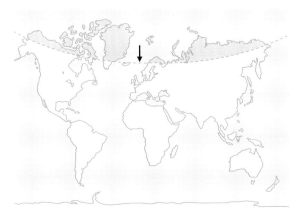

The Arctic Circle is marked with an arrow.

Climate, plants and animals

It is usually below freezing point (0 °C) in the Arctic. The sun does not rise for several months in winter so it is always dark. In summer, there is daylight all the time for several months. Some grasses, flowers, mosses and lichens grow in the land areas in the summer. Seals and walrus live in the seas. The biggest animals are polar bears, caribou and reindeer.

All of the land inside the Arctic Circle is tundra. During its very short summer, this land has many plants growing on it.

People in the Arctic

Some people live in countries that are in the Arctic region. They mostly hunt, fish, and herd reindeer. The first person reached the North Pole on 6 April 1909. This explorer was the American Robert Peary. In 1958, the US submarine *Nautilus* sailed in the ocean under the North Pole's ice cap.

Argentina

See also: South America

Argentina is a country on the southern tip of South America. Argentina has the high Andes Mountains and a long coast. It is the second largest country in South America.

Living and working

Argentina's cool grasslands are called the Pampas. They are very fertile. Farmers raise huge herds of cattle on the Pampas. Cowboys, called *gauchos*, ride on horses to herd the cattle.

Argentina also has many large, modern cities. 12 million people live in the capital, Buenos Aires. There are Spanish-style squares and buildings in many towns and cities. This is because Argentina was ruled by Spain until 1810.

Gauchos *move a herd of beef cattle across the Pampas.*

DID YOU KNOW?

Many of the highest peaks in the Andes are volcanoes. Some could erupt at any time.

Beef steak is Argentina's national dish. Restaurants serve giant helpings of steak, cooked over open grills.

SOUTH AMERICA

FACT FILE

PEOPLE	Argentines/ Argentinians
POPULATION	34.2 million
MAIN LANGUAGE	Spanish
CAPITAL CITY	Buenos Aires
MONEY	Peso
HIGHEST MOUNTAIN	Cerro Aconcagua – 6960 m
LONGEST RIVER	River Parana – 4500 km

Art

See also: Architecture, Painting, Sculpture

Art is painting, drawing, architecture and sculpture. Pictures and sculptures can show people, animals or things from the real world. This is called representational art. They can also show the ideas or the feelings of the artist, without being a picture of anything that is real. This kind of art is called abstract. Some art is a mixture of both.

How art developed

People have always made art. 15,000 years ago people made cave paintings using natural materials. Over the centuries many different materials have been used and many styles of art have developed. All of these use colours, lines, textures, patterns and shapes. Today, people can go to see works of art in art galleries or museums.

Vincent Van Gogh (1853–90)

Vincent Van Gogh was a very famous artist. He was born in the Netherlands. He did most of his painting in France. Van Gogh's paintings are still very popular. He used bright, deep colours and strong brush marks. Van Gogh painted many pictures of nature. He always signed his paintings with just his first name, 'Vincent'.

Van Gogh painted several nearly identical sunflower paintings. This one is in a museum in London.

Smooth texture

Curved lines

Warm, bronze colour

This abstract sculpture by the artist Naum Gabo was made in 1960.

Asia

See also: Continent

Asia is the biggest of the seven continents. It stretches from Europe in the west to the Pacific Ocean in the east. The islands of Japan and Indonesia are part of Asia.

The land

Throughout Asia there are great plains, which are flat, grassy areas. The world's highest mountain range, the Himalayas, is in Asia. Some of the most important rivers in the world, such as the Ganges and the Huang He, flow through Asia.

Climate, plants and animals

The north of Asia has freezing winters and cool summers. Pine forests grow where it is cold. Brown bears and wolves live in the forests. In the south and east, there is a hot and wet season and a warm and dry season. There are rainforests here. Monkeys, snakes and tigers live in the rainforests.

People in Asia

One-third of the people in the world live in Asia. Most of the people are farmers producing crops such as rice, wheat, tea and cotton. There are also many big cities with factories, business and shops.

ASIA FACTS

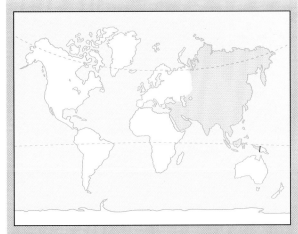

SIZE	45 million square km
HIGHEST MOUNTAIN	Mount Everest – 8848 m
LONGEST RIVER	Yangtse River – 5000 km
BIGGEST COUNTRY	China
SPECIAL FEATURE	Lake Baikal, the world's deepest lake – 1637 m deep

This is Hong Kong. It is one of the main business centres of Asia.

Australasia

See also: Aborigines, Continent, Marsupial

Australasia is one of the seven continents. It is sometimes called Oceania. Australia is the main land area. The rest of the continent is made up of 10,000 smaller islands. These include New Zealand and Papua New Guinea.

The land

Most of Australia is low and flat, except for the Great Dividing Range mountains. There are many kinds of islands in Australasia. Most are small and don't even have names.

Climate, plants and animals

The centre of Australia is a hot, dry desert. The north of Australia and parts of New Zealand and Papua New Guinea are hot and sometimes very wet. Australian animals include koalas, kangaroos, crocodiles and dingoes. The kiwi bird lives only in New Zealand.

People and countries

Most people in Australia and New Zealand live in towns and cities, and work in offices and factories. In the countryside, farmers raise cattle and sheep. People on the other islands of Australasia usually live on small farms or in fishing villages.

AUSTRALASIA FACTS

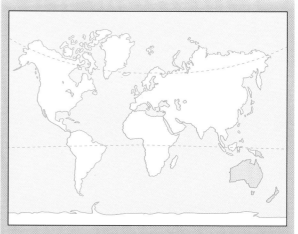

SIZE	8.6 million square km
HIGHEST MOUNTAIN	Mount Wilhelm in Papua New Guinea – 4508 m
LONGEST RIVER	Murray-Darling Rivers in Australia – 3750 km
BIGGEST COUNTRY	Australia
SPECIAL FEATURE	Uluru (Ayer's Rock), a big hill on a plain in Australia

This beach is on one of the Solomon Islands in the South Pacific.

Australia

See also: Aborigines, Australasia, Marsupial

Australia is a large country south-east of Asia. There are mountains in the east and hot, dry deserts in the centre and west. Hot, wet tropical forests are found in the north.

Living and working

The first people in Australia were the Aborigines. In the 1800s settlers came from Europe. Many Asian people have come to live in Australia. Australian culture is now a mix of all the traditions of the different Australians.

More than half of the people live in the cities. Factory workers process food and make machinery. There are millions of sheep and cattle grazing on huge farms called stations. One-third of all the world's wool comes from Australia's sheep.

This is the harbour in Sydney. Built out into the harbour, on the left, is the Sydney Opera House. It is famous for its modern architectural design.

DID YOU KNOW?

Some children live on remote sheep or cattle stations. They do not go to school. Instead they listen to the School of the Air, which is a kind of two-way radio school.

AUSTRALASIA

FACT FILE

PEOPLE	Australians
POPULATION	about 18 million
MAIN LANGUAGES	English, Aboriginal languages
CAPITAL CITY	Canberra
BIGGEST CITY	Sydney
MONEY	Australian dollar
HIGHEST MOUNTAIN	Mount Kosciusko – 2237 m
LONGEST RIVER	Murray-Darling Rivers – 3750 km

Austria

See also: Europe

Austria is a country in central Europe. It has many mountain ranges with wide valleys between them. The east of the country is flat. Winters are cold but the summers are warm.

Living and working

Most people live in small towns and villages. In the mountains, homes have steep, overhanging roofs. These keep the snow away from the house. Most of the world's graphite is mined in Austria. It is used to make pencil leads. Austria is famous for its special cakes and pastries. Every town and village has its own recipes. Austria is also very famous for its music. A music festival is held from May to June every year in Vienna.

These farm buildings near Innsbruck are made so the snow will slide off the roofs.

DID YOU KNOW?

The oldest school in Austria is in Vienna. It was opened by Benedictine monks 750 years ago.

Wolfgang Amadeus Mozart (1756–1791)

Mozart was a famous Austrian composer. He was already writing music by the time he was five years old. He died when he was only 35, but he had written over 600 pieces of music.

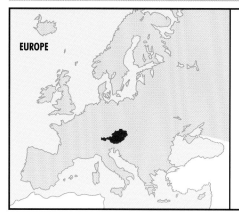

EUROPE

FACT FILE

PEOPLE...................... Austrians
POPULATION .... about 8 million
MAIN LANGUAGE........ German
CAPITAL CITY............. Vienna
MONEY...................... Schilling
HIGHEST MOUNTAIN... Grossglockner – 3797 m
LONGEST RIVER.......... River Danube – 2850 km

Aztecs

See also: Incas, Maya, Mexico

The Aztecs ruled part of Mexico about 600 years ago. They were a small group who grew by conquering their neighbours. The Aztecs took more and more land until they had a large empire.

What were the Aztecs like?

The Aztecs were ruled by a king. He had people who ran the country for him. There were also priests, warriors and traders. The ordinary people were farmers who grew crops in the fields and sold them at market.

The Aztecs believed that many gods and goddesses controlled the world. To keep them happy the Aztecs prayed and gave presents to the gods. Sometimes they even killed people for them.

This is an artist's idea of what the great Aztec city in Lake Texcoco, Tenochtitlan, would have looked like.

KEY DATES

1300 .... The first Aztecs settle by Lake Texcoco
1325 .... Tenochtitlan, a city in the middle of the lake, is built
1426–1515 ... The Aztec empire grows
1518 .... The Spanish reach Mexico
1519 .... The Spanish capture Tenochtitlan
1520 .... The Aztec civilization falls apart

What are the Aztecs famous for?

The Aztecs are famous for the beautiful gold jewellery and feather clothes that they made. They are also famous for their hieroglyphics (picture writing).

What happened to the Aztecs?

The Aztecs were beaten by the Spanish, led by Hernando Cortez, in 1519. Their empire fell apart. There are still people living in Mexico today who are directly related to the Aztecs.

Bacteria

See also: Virus

Bacteria are among the smallest living things. Bacteria live wherever they find food. Some bacteria make people and animals ill, but others are used to make cheese, yoghurt and some drugs.

How bacteria live

A bacterium has only one cell. There are no male or female bacteria. A bacterium divides into two cells to produce another bacterium just like itself. The number of bacteria can increase very quickly.

BACTERIA FACTS

SIZE .... 1,000,000 bacteria could fit on the head of a pin

LIFE SPAN .... up to 20 or more years

ENEMIES ...... antiseptics, antibiotics, white blood cells

Thick wall to cover and protect the bacterium

Soft jelly containing chemicals that break down food and build the cell

Thin hairs for swimming through liquids

A hipylori bacterium. It can cause bad tummy upsets. This bacteria is 10,400 times bigger than it really is.

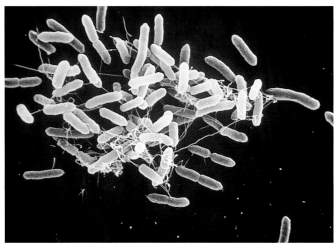

This photo of E. coli bacteria was taken through a microscope so the bacteria look 2500 times bigger than they really are. A person who studies bacteria is called a bacteriologist.

FOOD

Bacteria eat all kinds of food. Some bacteria help to break up dead plants, animals and other waste material.

Badger

See also: Mammal

The badger is a common mammal. It only comes out at night. Badgers can be found everywhere in Europe and across much of Asia. There is one kind of badger in North America.

FOOD

Badgers will eat almost anything they find, but their favourite foods are earthworms and small rodents.

BADGER FACTS

NUMBER
OF KINDS....8

COLOUR.....silvery grey, black and white

LENGTH......up to 95 cm

HEIGHT.......about 30 cm

WEIGHT......up to 16 kg

STATUS.......common

LIFE SPAN....15 years

ENEMIES......People hunt badgers with dogs. This is illegal. Many badgers are run over by cars.

Scent gland on the bottom to mark territory

Very sensitive nose

Short, stiff hair to protect the badger from thorns

Strong claws for digging and fighting

A Eurasian badger

Badger families

A male badger is called a boar and a female badger is called a sow. Female badgers give birth to up to seven cubs at a time. Badgers live in large families called groups. Each group digs a big network of tunnels called a sett. The adults bring fresh grass into the sett for bedding.

Three young Eurasian badgers out at night hunting through the leaves and soil for earthworms.

Bahamas

See also: Island, North America

The Bahamas is a country in the Caribbean. It has more than 700 small flat islands, and 2000 rocky mini islands. There are shallow seas all around them and many islands have white, sandy beaches. It is warm all year.

Living and working

Most people in the Bahamas live on one small island called New Providence. This is the centre of the tourist industry. Nearly everyone works with tourists, or fishes for a living. Because the soil is poor, it's hard to grow much food in the Bahamas. But tonnes of fish are caught, and everyone eats different fish dishes.

On the day after Christmas or on New Year's Day the Bahamas has a special festival called *Junkanoo*. There is music, and people wear masks and fantastic costumes. The streets are closed for parades and musical entertainment.

These fishermen sell what they catch directly from their boats at Potters Cay, Nassau, on New Providence Island.

DID YOU KNOW?

The Bahamas was once a hideout for pirates. The famous pirate Blackbeard lived on an island in the Bahamas.

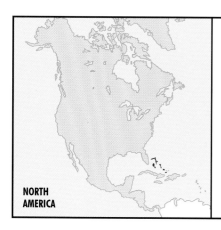

NORTH AMERICA

FACT FILE

PEOPLE .... Bahamians

POPULATION 272,000

MAIN LANGUAGES .... English, Creole

CAPITAL CITY .... Nassau

MONEY .... Bahamian dollar

HIGHEST MOUNTAIN ... Mount Alvernia – 206 m

Ballet

See also: Dance, Orchestra, Theatre

Ballet is a way of dancing that started in Europe in the mid-1600s. Both men and women can become ballet dancers. A ballet usually has special costumes, scenery and music. Most ballets tell a story. A person who creates a ballet is called a choreographer.

How a ballet is created

The choreographer plans the steps and positions the dancers use, and how they should show the story. The choreographer works with the dancers and the people who design the costumes and scenery. Usually the ballet is danced to music which has already been written, but sometimes new music is written for a ballet.

Training to be a ballet dancer is very hard work. It starts when the dancer is very young. Many children enjoy going to ballet classes just for fun, even if they do not want to become professional dancers.

The music for the ballet Swan Lake *was written by the Russian composer Tchaikovsky.*

DID YOU KNOW?

All ballet is based on five standing positions. The other special steps used in ballet all follow on from these five positions.

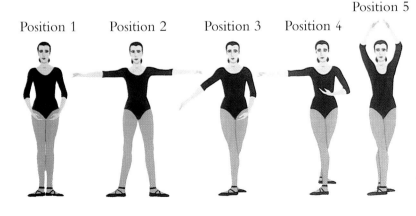

Position 1   Position 2   Position 3   Position 4   Position 5

These are the five basic positions in ballet.

Balloon

See also: Air, Transport

A balloon is a big bag filled with hot air or helium gas. Balloons were the first flying machines. They were invented more than a hundred years before aeroplanes.

The first balloons

In 1783 the French Montgolfier brothers made the first successful balloon. Early balloons floated wherever the wind took them. Later, giant cigar-shaped balloons called airships were built. These were filled with dangerous hydrogen gas. They had engines, could be steered and carried lots of passengers. But airships had many accidents because they could explode.

The first balloon lifts off in Paris in 1783. It was bright blue with gold designs.

How we use balloons

Modern balloons are much the same as the first ones, except they are made from lighter, stronger materials. Balloons are used by scientists to carry special instruments into the atmosphere, usually for checking the weather. Some people fly in balloons just for fun. They are too slow and unpredictable to be very useful as transport.

People travel in the baskets that hang down under these modern balloons.

BALLOON FACTS

FIRST INVENTED 1783
BIGGEST ....1939, an airship called
Graf Zepplin II

Bangladesh

See also: Asia

Bangladesh is in Asia. It has many rivers, with hills in the south-east. It is always very warm. Rain falls in the monsoon season when it is always wet and windy. This leads to floods which makes the soil good for farming.

DID YOU KNOW?

In Bangladesh, there is more travelling and transport along the rivers than along the roads. This is especially important during the floods in the monsoon season.

Living and working

Most people live in the countryside. Many houses are built on platforms. This stops the houses flooding in the monsoon season. Many people work on farms or catch fish. The plant, jute, is grown and made into sacks, rope and mats.

Bangladesh is famous for its fish curries. Mustard oil is used as a spicy flavouring.

These houses are raised on stilts along a river.

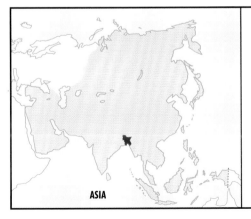

ASIA

FACT FILE

PEOPLE	Bangladeshi
POPULATION	about 123 million
MAIN LANGUAGES	Bengali, English
CAPITAL CITY	Dhaka
MONEY	Taka
HIGHEST MOUNTAIN	Mowdok Mual – 1003 m
LONGEST RIVER	River Ganges – 2510 km

Bar code

See also: Computer, Laser

A bar code is a pattern of black and white lines in a square or rectangular shape. Nearly everything that is sold has a bar code.

How bar codes work

At a supermarket checkout, the cashier moves each item across a scanner. The scanner has a glass window with a red criss-cross pattern on it. This pattern is light from a laser. When the light hits the white parts of the bar code it bounces off. Light does not bounce off the black lines.

A detector picks up the pattern and sends a message to a computer. The computer matches the code in its database to find out what is being scanned and how much it costs. The computer can add the price to the bill. The computer can print a receipt listing by name every item scanned.

Other uses for bar codes

Some shops and factories re-order supplies using bar codes. If a shelf looks empty, a bar code strip on the shelf is read by a bar code reader. This is then plugged into a computer, which prints an order. Many libraries use bar codes to record which books are taken out by their borrowers.

The shop assistant in this supermarket is checking the price of a carton of orange juice. He is using a special bar code scanner.

ISBN 0-435-02443-4

9 780435 024437

This is a bar code for a book. It can be used by a bookshop selling the book or by a warehouse where the books are stored.

Barbados

See also: Hurricane, North America

Barbados is a small island country in the Caribbean. It is tropical, which means it is very warm and wet all year round.

Living and working

Most people in Barbados live on the coast. They work with the people who come on holiday. There are sandy beaches and warm seas. Some Bajans are farmers. They grow sugar cane. Cutting the cane is hard, dirty work.

Every summer there is a festival called Cropover. It was first held in the days when many of the people were slaves, and were forced to work on sugar cane farms.

Today, Cropover is a chance for people to celebrate their freedom. They enjoy calypso music, dancing and parades. They make and eat special foods, such as fish cooked with spices and pepper.

Sugar cane is cut and stacked by hand. It goes to refineries where it is made into sugar products.

DID YOU KNOW?

Barbados is in the hurricane zone. These huge tropical storms can flatten everything, with winds of 250 kph.

NORTH AMERICA

FACT FILE

PEOPLE .... Bajans
POPULATION 261,000
MAIN LANGUAGES........ English, Creole
CAPITAL CITY .... Bridgetown
MONEY....................... Barbados dollar
HIGHEST MOUNTAIN.... Mount Hillaby – 333 m

Barge

See also: River, Transport, Waterway

A barge is a boat which can float in shallow water. Most barges have no mast or sails. They are towed or pushed. Barges are used on rivers and waterways.

The first barges

Barges were first used because it was easier to move large, heavy loads on water than on land. The first barges were pulled by horses. They carried coal and wood on rivers and on special waterways called canals. Engines took over from horses. Today some barges are towed or pushed by powerful boats called tugs.

How we use barges

Barges are still used to carry heavy loads, like coal, wood and stone. They can be seen on many of the world's big rivers. Often two or three at a time are hooked together and towed, like wagons on a train.

DID YOU KNOW?

Some old barges have been converted into floating houses. People live on them, or have holidays on the rivers and canals.

A horse-drawn barge in the early 1800s in England.

This string of barges is on the Mississippi River in the USA. They are being pushed by a tug boat.

Bat

See also: Mammal

Bats are the only mammals that can fly. Most bats fly at night. They avoid crashing into things by making high noises that bounce off objects to give echoes. The echoes help bats to find their way in the dark. Bats live in all parts of the world except the Arctic and Antarctic.

BAT FACTS

NUMBER OF KINDS	more than 2000
COLOUR	black, brown, grey or yellow
WINGSPAN	usually 20–30 cm
WEIGHT	usually 5–40 g
STATUS	common
LIFE SPAN	15–25 years
ENEMIES	cats, owls, foxes, skunks, snakes

FOOD

Most bats eat either fruit or flying insects. Some eat larger animals, such as lizards and scorpions. A bat may eat half its own weight of food every night.

Wings of thin skin stretched between the bat's long fingers

Back feet with claws for hanging upside-down

Large ears to catch echoes of the high-pitched squeaks that it makes

Fur to keep warm

Sharp teeth chew up food

A greater horseshoe bat

Bat families

Some bats live alone, but others live in groups called colonies. Female bats usually have only one baby at a time. After the mother gives birth to her baby, she joins with other female bats to look after the young bats in a special nursery colony. A bat always returns to the same cave, building or tree to sleep. Many bats fly to a different cave to hibernate for the winter.

This bat is hanging upside-down while it eats a piece of fruit. Some bats also hang upside down to sleep.

Bay

See also: Coast, Ocean, Port

A bay is formed where the coastline curves in, usually making a shape like half a circle. Bays are found all over the world and are of many different sizes. The Bay of Biscay, off France, is 500 km wide. Very small bays are called coves. Some deep bays are used as harbours for boats.

How a bay is formed

A bay is made when waves wear away the coast. The sea wears away soft rock faster than hard rock. The bay is made when soft rock is washed away over a long period of time.

Headlands are formed by the harder rock at the ends of the bay. Waves wash sand and pebbles into the bay, onto the beach.

People and bays

The water in small bays is usually calm and shallow. This makes it safe for boats and for swimming. Cities and sea ports are often built on the edge of bays. The Californian city of San Francisco in the United States is nicknamed the 'city on the bay'.

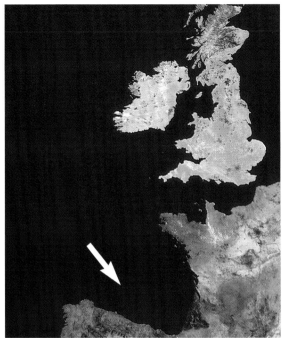

The arrow points towards the Bay of Biscay off the coasts of France and Spain.

Lulworth Cove is a small bay with a very narrow entrance to the sea. It is in Dorset on the south coast of England.

DID YOU KNOW?

The Bay of Bengal in the Indian Ocean is the world's biggest bay. It is 1600 km wide.

Bear

See also: Mammal

Bears are very strong and powerful mammals. Bears live over most of the northern hemisphere. The biggest bear is the polar bear. The smallest is the sun bear.

FOOD

Most bears eat many different kinds of food, such as nuts, berries, fish and fruit. The polar bear eats mostly seals.

BEAR FACTS

NUMBER
OF KINDS.....7
COLOUR..... black, brown, red, bluish, white or cream
LENGTH...... 1.3–3 m
HEIGHT....... 90 cm to 1.6 m
WEIGHT...... 50–650 kg
STATUS........ some are threatened
LIFE SPAN.... around 25 years
ENEMIES...... People hunt bears for their fur. Cubs may be eaten by wolves.

Thick fur to keep warm

Good sense of smell to find food

Long legs for running and walking

Strong claws for digging and climbing trees

A polar bear

Bear families

A male bear is called a he-bear and a female bear is called a she-bear. Bear babies are called cubs. Cubs live with their mother for one or two years, but then move away. The male bears live on their own and the females start to have their own cubs. A bear's home is called a den. Usually this is dug in the earth or snow by the adult bear. A mother and her one or two cubs will stay in their den for the whole winter. In very cold places, some bears hibernate for most of the winter.

A female brown bear and her cubs.

Beaver

See also: Mammal

The beaver is a mammal. It has webbed feet, a big flat tail and gnaws down trees to build dams in water to make its home. There are two kinds – the American beaver and the European beaver (now found only in Poland).

FOOD

Beavers like to eat the wood just beneath tree bark, but will also eat water plants, thistles, tree roots, twigs and seeds.

BEAVER FACTS

NUMBER
OF KINDS.... 2
COLOUR..... brown
LENGTH...... up to 170 cm
HEIGHT....... up to 60 cm
WEIGHT...... up to 30 kg
STATUS........ common
LIFE SPAN.... 20 years
ENEMIES...... bears and wolves
Some people hunt beavers for their fur.

The beaver's fur is almost waterproof and good for swimming under water

An American beaver

Nose and ears can be closed for diving

Sharp teeth are used to cut down trees

Large, flat tail for swimming and for slapping the water to warn of danger

Big webbed back feet are used for swimming

Beaver families

A beaver family consists of two parents, and the babies born during the past two years. A pair of beavers may have up to eight babies called kits, in a year. A beaver family's home is called a lodge. It is made out of logs and mud. Its entrances are under the water. If the water is not deep enough to build a safe lodge the beavers build a dam to make the water deeper.

An adult American beaver strips the bark off a branch, watched by a beaver kit.

Bee

See also: Insect, Wasp

A bee is an insect which makes honey. Honey bees make the most honey. Bee-keepers keep honey bees in special boxes, called hives. Bees live in all parts of the world except the Arctic and Antarctic.

BEE FACTS

NUMBER OF KINDS....	20,000
COLOUR.....	black to light brown
LENGTH......	usually 1–2cm
STATUS........	common
LIFE SPAN....	up to 5 years
ENEMIES......	people, bears, honey badgers, birds, ants, wasps

FOOD

A bee feeds on nectar and the powdery pollen from the stamens of flowers. Nectar is a sugary juice from flowers, which bees make into honey.

Wings to move in all directions so it can fly forwards, backwards, sideways and even hover

Two large eyes and three small eyes to see all around

Antennae to smell and to touch

Pollen baskets store pollen inside long, curved hairs

Sting to pump poison into enemies

A honey bee

Bee families

Honey bees and bumble bees live in large groups called colonies. Each colony has three kinds of bee. One large female, called the queen bee, lays eggs. Other female bees are workers who collect food and look after the queen, the hive and the young. Drones are male bees who mate with the queen.

Honey bees make a waxy honeycomb. The queen bee lays thousands of eggs, each in a different cell in the honeycomb.

Beetle

See also: Insect, Ladybird

Beetles are the most common kinds of insect. Beetles live all over the world, except in the sea. Some beetles damage crops, such as potatoes and cotton. Other beetles help to get rid of dead plants and animals.

FOOD

Beetles eat plants and insects. Some feed on rotting plants and dead animals.

BEETLE FACTS

NUMBER OF KINDS	....about 300,000
COLOUR	.....usually black, brown or dark red
LENGTH	......0.5 mm to 13 cm
WEIGHT	.....up to 40 g
STATUS	.... common
LIFE SPAN	...usually less than a year
ENEMIES	...... birds, lizards, snakes, other insects

Strong jaws chew through food

Antennae smell food

Tiny holes in body for breathing

Hard wing covers protect the wings when the beetle is not flying

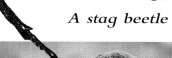

A stag beetle

Beetle families

Most beetles live on their own. A beetle starts life as an egg laid on a leaf or in a crack. The egg hatches into a grub which usually looks like a small worm. The grub changes into a pupa which looks a bit like the adult. The pupa usually lives underground until it changes into an adult.

The dung beetle clears away animal dung by rolling it into a ball and pushing it away.

Belgium

See also: Europe

Belgium is a country in north-west Europe. There is flat land around the coast. The Ardennes highlands in the south-east are hot in summer and cold in winter. There is a central plain.

Living and working

Most Belgians live in towns and cities. Some people in Belgium work making cars and textiles. Farmers grow flax which is made into cloth called linen. Some people work in coal mines.

Belgium is famous for its special, luxury chocolates. They are now sold all over the world.

Belgium has many festivals, especially during February. A three-day carnival is held at the town of Binche. Everyone wears bright costumes and the men dress in high, plumed hats.

This flower market is in the Grand Place in the Belgian capital, Brussels.

DID YOU KNOW?

Brussels, the capital of Belgium, is the headquarters of the European Union (EU) and the North Atlantic Treaty Organization (NATO).

EUROPE

FACT FILE

PEOPLE......................Belgians
POPULATION..............about 10 million
MAIN LANGUAGES.......Flemish, French
CAPITAL CITY.............Brussels
MONEY.....................Belgian franc
HIGHEST MOUNTAIN...Botrange – 649 m
LONGEST RIVER..........River Schelde – 435 km

Belize

See also: Maya, North America

Belize is a small country on the Caribbean coast of Central America. The coast is swampy. Away from the sea there are mountains and forests. Belize is always warm and wet.

Living and working

On the coast of Belize people live in wooden houses built up on stilts to keep the houses dry. Away from the coast, the houses, have roofs of banana leaves from the banana trees that grow all around.

This is a dock where the fishing and tourist boats land at San Pedro Town.

Inland, farmers grow a kind of maize, like sweetcorn. They grind it into flour, and make flat pancakes called tortillas.

Belizian cooking is called Creole. It is a spicy mixture of tastes from the Caribbean and Africa.

DID YOU KNOW?

Mayan Indians live in Belize. You can still see the ancient ruins of temples built by their ancestors.

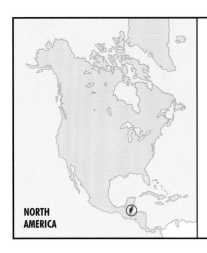

NORTH AMERICA

FACT FILE

PEOPLE .... Belizians

POPULATION 210,000

MAIN LANGUAGES .... English, Creole and Spanish

CAPITAL CITY .... Belmopan

LARGEST CITY .... Belize City

MONEY .... Belize dollar

HIGHEST MOUNTAIN ... Victoria Peak – 1122 m

LONGEST RIVER .... Belize River – 290 km

Bicycle

See also: Motorcycle, Transport

A bicycle is a machine with two wheels. When the two pedals are pushed, the wheels go round.

The first bicycles

The first bicycles were not meant for transportation. They were invented for rich people and were used for fun and exercise. They had no pedals or brakes. Riders just sat on the bicycle seat and ran along the ground. Gradually new inventions were added, such as soft tyres. Today bicycles have gears that make pedalling easier. Bicycles are light and strong, made from plastic or metal.

Why people use bicycles

Bicycles are cheap, and much faster than walking. Bicycles are used today for sport, exercise and fun. In many countries, such as China, they are the most important form of transport. Everyone uses bicycles. There are bicycles to carry luggage, and even bicycle taxis.

BICYCLE FACTS

FIRST	1791: the first pedal-less 'Hobby horse', Paris 1839: first pedal bicycle built by Kirkpatrick Macmillan, Scotland
BIGGEST	seats 35 people
FASTEST	87.6 kph

The penny-farthing bicycle was not easy to ride. It was only popular for a short time in the late 1800s.

The bicycle is a very popular form of transport in China.

Bird

See also: Animal, Seabird

Birds are animals with feathers, a beak and wings. All birds hatch from eggs, but not all birds can fly. Birds live all over the world. A person who studies birds is called an ornithologist.

Bird families

A female bird is often called a hen. A male bird is often called a cock. Young birds are called chicks and they hatch from eggs laid by the mother. Most birds build a nest to protect the eggs and chicks until the chicks are old enough to take care of themselves. Some birds live together in groups called flocks.

BIRD FACTS

BIGGEST	............the ostrich – over 150 kg
SMALLEST	...........the humming bird – less than 2 g
BEST SWIMMER	....the penguin
FASTEST	..............the swift – up to 130 kph

A thin beak is good for catching insects.

A sharp, hooked beak is good for tearing meat.

A short wide beak with a point is good for cracking seeds and small nuts.

A bird's beak is shaped to suit the kind of food it eats. Birds use their beaks to pick up things, as well as to eat.

The individual spines of a feather are held together with tiny hooks.

Only birds have feathers. Thick feathers help to keep the bird warm in cold areas. The colours of the feathers can help a bird hide from enemies or attract a mate.